A Special

# Glossary

Of

# Healing Stones

## Plus Birthstones

Robert W. Wood D.Hp
(Diploma in Hypnotherapy)

Rosewood Publishing

First published in U.K. 2001
By Rosewood Publishing
P.O. Box 219, Huddersfield,
West Yorkshire HD2 2YT

www.rosewood-gifts.co.uk

Copy-editing
Margaret Wakefield BA (Hons) London
www.euroreportage.co.uk

Cover photograph by
Andrew Caveney BA (Hons)
www.andrewcaveneyphotography.co.uk

Cover and layout re-designed by
AJ Typesetting
www.ajtype.co.uk

Printed in Great Britain by
Delta Design & Print Ltd
www.deltaleeds.co.uk

ISBN 978-0-9532930-1-8                                              BK2

# CRYSTAL HEALING

**The source of Love, Protection, Health and Security which we all seek comes from a UNIVERSAL LIFE FORCE which we often call God. To receive such a gift and have it work for us, we have to value it by listening, and then responding with our willingness to receive it.**

## How do we receive? ... Through the mind.

If prayer is the asking, then meditation is the listening - and Mother Nature has produced some wonderful tools, in the form of Gemstones and Crystals, to help us to receive the answers to our constant requests for help.

How strange, though, that we have such wonderful minds that can so easily appreciate the natural beauty of earth's abundance on the one hand, and yet, on the other hand, this same mind seems - even when we don't want it to be - distracted, easily wandering off from one subject to another. How easily we seem to catch irrational fears and phobias ... How difficult for us to change, even though we want to.

How fearful a new day can become ...
Why is it that, for no known reason, we get feelings of unease, distress and even confusion?

Why is it that things seem to go wrong?

One answer seems to be: 'It's simply the way we are.'

Luckily, life doesn't want things to go wrong, nor for us to be out of balance with Nature, and fortunately seems to have produced many ways to help restore our *natural, intended state of balance.*

However, there may be a paradox here, in that the very thing we search for, we may already have. That is: built in to the **life force** is the ability to *heal*, to *change*, and to *discover* for ourselves a state of mind often referred to as ... *Peace of Mind.*

The most precious Crystal of all is ... OURSELVES.

*So why not TURN IT ON and TUNE IT IN?*

**Prayer** ..... is the **Asking**

**Meditation** ..... is the **Listening**

**Crystals** ..... are the **Tools for the Job**

This booklet deals with the tools: *Gemstones & Crystals.*

Although it's impossible to know in advance, one thing you can be sure of when using crystals is - that change will come.

Crystals are like amplifiers and transformers of energy. The smallest thought can be immediately enlarged by a crystal.

Crystals are tools, so it's not so much the Crystal that will do the work, but more the person who holds it, who can channel the energy for Change ... Healing **through** the Crystal.

Through the centuries man has used Crystals to treat many ailments and conditions. Ancient and Medieval records show that Crystals have been used to bring about remarkable results.

A very easy demonstration of the power held within Crystals is to simply take two quartz crystals such as Rock Crystal or Rose Quartz, or even Amethyst, no bigger than a small coin, and rub them together in the dark - and you'll see them spectacularly light up.

The mind is even more exciting. Just look at the picture of the staircase on the next page for a while - and when it moves, you'll be astounded by the effect!

# THE SHIFTING STAIRCASE

In searching for connections within the mind, you need go no further than this picture. You will know what I mean if you just stare at it for no more than 20 seconds.

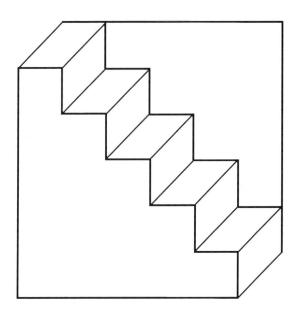

When you first look, you may see the staircase as if you were standing at the bottom right hand corner of the picture, ready to walk up the steps; then it will change, almost as if by magic, so that you are now in the bottom left hand corner, underneath the steps - or vice versa.

This change occurs in a fraction of a second, and it's this *change* that holds the key. **It's this *'change'* that, when connected to the stones, will bring about the desired *'life changing effects'*.**

*The **power** that created this effect is the **same power** that helps you to* **connect**.

## Life is a journey - so enjoy the journey!

There are a number of other interesting pictures and a fuller explanation of how to use this natural effect with amazing results in my book, 'Discover Why Crystal Healing Works'. Here I am only dealing with the Glossary of Healing Stones.

The simplest way to use Crystals is for you to be connected to your chosen Gemstone or Crystal. This can be done in many ways, and all the different ways are intended to help you to connect mentally.

Effort of some kind has to be employed. If you bought a Crystal, brought it home, put it into a drawer and forgot about it, then the opportunity would have been missed and you would have wasted your money.

One of the simplest ways to connect is by holding the Crystal, or wearing it in the form of jewellery. Or you can use visualisation - hold the Crystal, and imagine a white light covering you and it.

Burying the Crystal in the ground enables it to be re-energised. To cleanse a Crystal, put it under a running water tap and allow it to dry naturally. The more you do, the more effective the outcome seems to be!

All these rituals ... and there are so many more; for example, you could produce an Elixir and take a sip every night just before going to bed, or first thing in the morning. You could wrap the stone in silk and leave it under your pillow. My mother has a piece of Amethyst under her pillow to help her sleep. I carry a piece of Green Aventurine in my money pocket, because it's said to be a money magnet.

In fact, your only limits are the limits of your own imagination!

**In your search, may you find the Truth.**

# Glossary of Healing Stones

You may believe it's **God's Power**, or brought about by a **Universal Life Force**, or just simply derived from a natural state of **evolution**. I believe that the *Power to Heal* can be found within the mind, and more importantly in the **imagination**.

So the following list has been compiled using combinations of either two or three Gemstones-Crystals (rather than singles as often found in other publications), because combinations can have a very positive and powerful effect within our minds.

The following information **is not authoritative**, but is a fluid interpretation drawn from many sources.

*PRECAUTIONARY WARNING: It is always advisable to consult your own Doctor before embarking on any course of self-treatment or using any type of alternative therapy.*

*NB: On no account should a Gemstone or Crystal ever be swallowed.*

# A

| | |
|---|---|
| **Aches & Pains** (easing of) | Rose Quartz, Rock Crystal & Hematite |
| **Abdominal Colic** | Mother of Pearl & Obsidian Snowflake |
| **Accidents** (prevention of) | Yellow Carnelian & Tiger Eye |
| **Addiction** | Amethyst & Black Onyx |
| **Adults Only** (aphrodisiac) | Rose Quartz, Amethyst & Carnelian |
| **Acidity** | Green Jasper & Rock Crystal |
| **Ageing** (to retard general process of) | 'Elixir of Life' Sodalite & Rhodonite |
| **Aggression** (moderation of) | Carnelian & Amethyst |
| **Alcoholism** | Amethyst & Black Onyx |
| **Allergies** | Red Jasper, Rock Crystal & Carnelian |
| **Anaemia** | Citrine & Hematite |
| **Anger** | Carnelian & Amethyst |
| **Angina** | Rose Quartz & Amethyst |

| | |
|---|---|
| **Animals** (to cure illnesses) | Rose Quartz & Rock Crystal |
| **Anorexia** | Rhodochrosite & Rose Quartz |
| **Anxiety** | Rock Crystal & Tiger Eye |
| **Arthritis** | Mother of Pearl & Carnelian |
| | *also* Copper & Magnets |
| **Asthma** | Amber & Rose Quartz |

# B

| | |
|---|---|
| **Backache** | Blue Agate & Hematite |
| **Bad Temper** | Blue Tiger Eye & Green Aventurine |
| **Baldness** | Aquamarine & Rock Crystal |
| **Bladder** | Jade & Red Jasper |
| **Bleeding** | Bloodstone & Carnelian |
| **Blood Circulation** | Sodalite & Carnelian |
| **Blood Pressure** (high) | Jade & Sodalite |
| **Blood Pressure** (low) | Sodalite & Carnelian |
| **Brain Tonic** | Amethyst & Carnelian |
| **Breathlessness** | Amber & Black Onyx |
| **Bronchitis** | Amber & Black Onyx |
| **Bruises** | Rose Quartz & Carnelian |
| **Burns** | Sodalite & Amethyst |

# C

| | |
|---|---|
| **Calming** | Sodalite & Rock Crystal |
| **Cancer** | Red Jasper, Rock Crystal & Carnelian |
| **Catarrh** | Amber & Blue Agate |
| **Cell Rejuvenation** | Sodalite & Rhodonite |
| **Central Nervous System** | Rock Crystal & Rose Quartz |
| **Chest Pains** | Malachite & Rose Quartz |
| **Circulation** | Sodalite & Carnelian |
| **Concentration** | Carnelian & Red Jasper |
| **Constipation** | Red Jasper & Citrine |
| **Coughs** | Aquamarine & Blue Agate |
| **Courage** | Hematite & Tiger Eye |

| Cramp | Bloodstone & Amethyst |
| Creativity | Amethyst & Red Jasper |
| Crown Energy | Rock Crystal & Amethyst |

# D

| Depression (to lift) | Tiger Eye, Carnelian & Hematite |
| Despair | Rhodonite & Carnelian |
| Diabetes | Rock Crystal & Red Jasper |
| Digestion | Citrine & Obsidian Snowflake |
| Dreams | Rutilated Quartz & Jade |
| Drunkenness | Amethyst & Tiger Eye |

# E

| Ear Problems | Amethyst & Blue Agate |
| Eczema | Amethyst & Green Aventurine |
| Elixir of Life | Rhodonite & Sodalite |
| Emotional Strength | Amethyst & Rose Quartz |
| Energy Booster | Amethyst, Rock Crystal & Carnelian |
| Epilepsy | Black Onyx & Tourmaline |
| Eyesight | Obsidian Snowflake & Rose Quartz |

# F

| Fainting | Amethyst & Lapis Lazuli |
| Fatigue | Amethyst, Rock Crystal & Carnelian |
| Fear | Rose Quartz & Rhodonite |
| Fertility | Rock Crystal, Rose Quartz & Moonstone |
| Fever | Carnelian & Red Jasper |
| Forgetfulness | Rhodonite & Unakite |
| Fractures | Mother of Pearl & Hematite |
| Frustration | Obsidian Clear & Rose Quartz |

# G

| Gall Bladder | Red Jasper & Tiger Eye |
| General Tonic | Green Aventurine & Blue Agate |

| | |
|---|---|
| **Good Luck** | Moonstone, Green Aventurine & Obsidian Snowflake |
| **Grief** | Red Jasper & Obsidian Clear |

# H

| | |
|---|---|
| **Haemorrhoids** | Mother of Pearl & Obsidian Clear |
| **Hair** | Aquamarine & Rock Crystal |
| **Happiness** | Carnelian & Sodalite |
| **Hay Fever** | Amber & Tiger Eye |
| **Headache** | Rose Quartz & Hematite |
| **Hearing** | Blue Agate & Rhodonite |
| **Heart Disease** | Rock Crystal, Red Jasper & Carnelian |
| **Hypochondria** | Tiger Eye & Blue Agate |

# I

| | |
|---|---|
| **Imagine** (a key to Life) | Rose Quartz, Green Aventurine & Amethyst |
| **Immune System** | Blue Agate & Carnelian |
| **Impotence** | Rhodonite & Sodalite |
| **Indigestion** | Jasper & Citrine |
| **Insomnia** | Amethyst & Sodalite |
| **Intestine** | Mother of Pearl & Obsidian Snowflake |
| **Intuition** | Amethyst & Rock Crystal |
| **Irritated Throat** | Amber & Rhodonite |
| **Itching** | Green Aventurine & Hematite |

# K

| | |
|---|---|
| **Kidney** | Jade & Carnelian |
| **Knees** | Mother of Pearl & Blue Agate |
| **Knowledge** | Amethyst & Rock Crystal |

# L

| | |
|---|---|
| **Laryngitis** | Amber & Rhodonite |
| **Laziness** | Hematite & Blue Agate |
| **Liver** | Rhodonite & Jasper |

| | |
|---|---|
| **Loneliness** | Rhodochrosite & Amethyst |
| **Longevity** | Sodalite & Rhodonite |
| **Love** (potion) | Rose Quartz & Amethyst |
| **Lungs** | Fluorite & Amber |

# M

| | |
|---|---|
| **Melancholy** | Red Jasper & Carnelian |
| **Memory** | Rhodonite & Unakite |
| **Menopause** | Moonstone & Rose Quartz |
| **Menstrual Cycle** | Carnelian & Moonstone |
| **Migraine** | Rose Quartz & Obsidian Clear |
| **Mouth** | Sodalite & Tiger Eye |
| **Multiple Sclerosis** | Red Jasper, Rock Crystal & Carnelian) |
| **Muscles** | Rock Crystal & Hermatite |

# N

| | |
|---|---|
| **Nails** | Rhodochrosite & Mother of Pearl |
| **Neck** (tension) | Hematite & Rose Quartz |
| **Negative Energy** (to dispel) | Lapis Lazuli & Obsidian Snowflake |
| **Nervousness** | Rhodonite & Mother of Pearl |
| **Neuralgia** | Rose Quartz & Hematite |
| **Nightmares** | Amethyst & Rhodonite |

# O

| | |
|---|---|
| **Obesity** | Black Onyx & Rock Crystal |
| **Obsessions** | Blue Agate & Black Onyx |

# P

| | |
|---|---|
| **Pain** (to relieve) | Rose Quartz, Rock Crystal & Hematite |
| **Paralysis** | Amethyst & Rock Crystal |
| **Patience** | Rock Crystal & Howlite |
| **Peace of Mind** | Green Aventurine, Rose Quartz & Rhodonite |
| **Phobias** | Obsidian Clear & Rose Quartz |

| | |
|---|---|
| **Pregnancy** (for strength) | Hematite & Carnelian |
| **Prosperity** | Green Aventurine & Obsidian Snowflake |
| **Protection** | Tiger Eye & Obsidian Snowflake |
| **Public Speaking** | Amber & Tiger Eye |

# Q

| | |
|---|---|
| **Quarrelling** (between couples) | Rose Quartz, Green Aventurine & Rhodonite |

# R

| | |
|---|---|
| **Red Blood Cells** (to promote health) | Hematite & Amethyst |
| **Rejuvenator** | Sodalite & Rhodonite |
| **Reproductive System** | Rose Quartz & Moonstone |
| **Rheumatism** | Mother of Pearl & Carnelian *also* Copper & Magnets |

# S

| | |
|---|---|
| **Sadness** | Sodalite & Red Jasper |
| **Scar Tissue** | Rose Quartz & Rock Crystal |
| **Sciatica** | Rose Quartz & Hematite |
| **Serenity** | Rock Crystal & Rhodonite |
| **Sexual Appetite** (to arouse & increase) | Rose Quartz, Amethyst & Carnelian |
| **Shyness** | Tiger Eye & Hematite |
| **Sinus** | Sodalite & Black Onyx |
| **Skin Problems** | Green Aventurine & Rose Quartz |
| **Sleep** | Amethyst & Howlite |
| **Smell** (to improve sense of) | Red Jasper & Tiger Eye |
| **Sores** | Green Aventurine & Amethyst |
| **Speech** | Rhodonite & Blue Agate |
| **Stamina** | Amethyst, Rock Crystal & Carnelian |
| **Stomach** | Mother of Pearl & Obsidian Snowflake |
| **Stress** | Green Aventurine, Rose Quartz & Rhodonite |

# T

| | |
|---|---|
| **Teeth** | Mother of Pearl & Calcite |
| **Tension** | Rose Quartz & Carnelian |
| **Throat** | Blue Agate & Amber |
| **Thyroid** | Rhodonite & Lapis Lazuli |
| **Tiredness** | Amethyst, Rose Quartz & Carnelian |
| **Tumours** | Amethyst & Rose Quartz |

# U

| | |
|---|---|
| **Ulcers** | Green Aventurine & Tiger Eye |
| **Urinary System** | Citrine & Jade |

# V

| | |
|---|---|
| **Varicose Veins** | Aquamarine & Rhodonite |
| **Vertigo** | Red Jasper & Obsidian Clear |
| **Vocal Cords** | Rhodonite & Blue Agate |

# W

| | |
|---|---|
| **Wasting Disease** | Red Jasper, Rock Crystal & Carnelian |
| **Weak Muscles** | Amethyst, Rock Crystal & Hematite |
| **Weakness** *(general)* | Amethyst, Rock Crystal & Hematite |
| **Will Power** | Rose Quartz, Black Onyx & Rock Crystal |
| **Wisdom** | Amethyst & Carnelian |
| **Wounds** | Rose Quartz & Rock Crystal |

# Live the Journey - the Journey is Life

**If thinking is the rocket**
**Then believing is the propellant**

**If thinking is the birth of the desire**
**Then believing makes the connection to the**
**Power that makes it happen**

## Look at things not as they are, but as they can be.

You can accomplish almost anything if you **believe** you can. We all have **God-given** talents and abilities, if only we could learn how to use them.

Keep an open mind ... for many, Crystal Healing works and has proved to be very beneficial, so discover for yourself if you can be one of those people that can benefit.

See your local stockist for any Gemstones and Crystals mentioned in this publication.

However, if you are having difficulty in obtaining any of the stones mentioned, we do offer our own mail order service and would be more than pleased to supply any of the stones listed.

Most Gemstones and Crystals, with just a few exceptions - for example Mother of Pearl - can be supplied in the form of Tumblestones. These are smooth, rounded stones, ideal for use as a Birthstone or as Healing Crystals. The nature of Mother of Pearl, and one or two others, prevents them being supplied as Tumblestones; however, we would be pleased to supply these in their natural forms.

For further details - write to:
ROSEWOOD,
P.O. Box 219, Huddersfield, West Yorkshire, HD2 2YT.

E-mail enquiries to: info@rosewood-gifts.co.uk

Or why not visit our website for even more information:

## www.rosewood-gifts.co.uk

For your convenience, all the Gemstones and Crystals mentioned in this *Special Glossary of Healing Stones* are listed alphabetically below.

| | | | |
|---|---|---|---|
| 1 | Amber | 18 | Magnets |
| 2 | Amethyst | 19 | Malachite |
| 3 | Aquamarine | 20 | Moonstone |
| 4 | Black Onyx | 21 | Mother of Pearl |
| 5 | Bloodstone | 22 | Obsidian Clear |
| 6 | Blue Agate | 23 | Obsidian Snowflake |
| 7 | Blue Tiger Eye | 24 | Red Jasper |
| 8 | Carnelian | 25 | Rhodochrosite |
| 9 | Citrine | 26 | Rhodonite |
| 10 | Copper | 27 | Rock Crystal |
| 11 | Fluorite | 28 | Rose Quartz |
| 12 | Green Aventurine | 29 | Rutilated Quartz |
| 13 | Green Jasper | 30 | Sodalite |
| 14 | Hematite | 31 | Tiger Eye |
| 15 | Howlite | 32 | Tourmaline |
| 16 | Jade | 33 | Unakite |
| 17 | Lapis Lazuli | 34 | Yellow Jasper |

# BIRTHSTONES

There are beliefs that Birthstones can have an influence or bearing on our lives. It is explained that our bodies reverberate to celestial vibrations, and that throughout our lives we have this 'vibration' of our ruling planets within our bodies. Never is this planetary influence so strong as at the time of our birth.

Using the appropriate Birthstone seems to contribute to putting us more closely in line with the energies of our astrological sign and its ruling planet.

It is believed that Birthstones were originally given to the new-born, maybe in the form of a pendant or a loose stone, so as to protect the child from harm and help attract and bring about good luck.

There are many Gemstones and Crystals associated with the Star Signs. After extensive research, this is my list.


### ARIES                                    Red Jasper
The Ram
21 March - 20 April


### TAURUS                                 Rose Quartz
The Bull
21 April - 21 May


### GEMINI                                  Black Onyx
The Twins
22 May - 21 June


### CANCER                               Mother of Pearl
The Crab
22 June - 22 July

## LEO
The Lion
23 July - 23 August

**Tiger Eye**

## VIRGO
The Virgin
24 August - 22 September

**Carnelian**

## LIBRA
The Scales
23 September - 23 October

**Green Aventurine**

## SCORPIO
The Scorpion
24 October - 22 November

**Rhodonite**

## SAGITTARIUS
The Archer or Centaur
23 November - 21 December

**Sodalite**

## CAPRICORN
The Goat
22 December - 20 January

**Obsidian Snowflake**

## AQUARIUS
The Water-Carrier
21 January - 19 February

**Blue Agate**

## PISCES
The Fish
20 February - 20 March

**Amethyst**

*Other titles in the 'POWER FOR LIFE' series:*

**Discover your own Special Birthstone and the renowned Healing Powers of Crystals** REF. (BK1) A look at Birthstones, personality traits and characteristics associated with each Sign of the Zodiac – plus a guide to the author's own unique range of Power Gems.

**Create a Wish Kit using a Candle, a Crystal and the Imagination of Your Mind** REF. (BK3) 'The key to happiness is having dreams; the key to success is making dreams come true.' This book will help you achieve.

**Gemstone & Crystal Elixirs – Potions for Love, Health, Wealth, Energy and Success** REF. (BK4) An ancient form of 'magic', invoking super-natural powers. You won't believe the power you can get from a drink!

**Crystal Pendulum for Dowsing** REF. (BK5) An ancient knowledge for unlocking your Psychic Power, to seek out information not easily available by any other means. Contains easy-to-follow instructions.

**Crystal Healing – Fact or Fiction? Real or Imaginary?** REF. (BK6) Find the answer in this book. Discover a hidden code used by Jesus Christ for healing, and read about the science of light and colour. It's really amazing.

**How to Activate the Hidden Power in Gemstones and Crystals** REF. (BK7) The key is to energise the thought using a crystal. The conscious can direct – but discover the real power. It's all in this book.

**Astrology: The Secret Code** REF. (BK8) In church it's called 'Myers Briggs typology'. In this book it's called 'psychological profiling'. If you read your horoscope, you need to read this to find your true birthstone.

**Talismans, Charms and Amulets** REF. (BK9) Making possible the powerful transformations which we would not normally feel empowered to do without a little extra help. Learn how to make a lucky talisman.

**A Guide to the Mysteries surrounding Gemstones & Crystals** REF. (BK10) Crystal healing, birthstones, crystal gazing, lucky talismans, elixirs, crystal dowsing, astrology, rune stones, amulets and rituals.

**A Simple Guide to Gemstone & Crystal Power – a mystical A-Z of stones** REF. (BK11) From Agate to Zircon, all you ever needed or wanted to know about the mystical powers of gemstones and crystals.

**Change Your Life by Using the Most Powerful Crystal on Earth** REF. (BK12) The most powerful crystal on earth can be yours. A book so disarmingly simple to understand, yet with a tremendous depth of knowledge.

All the above books are available from your local stockist,
or, if not, from the publisher.

# NOTES

# Welcome to the world of Rosewood

An extract from a 'thank- you' letter for one of my books.

*"I realised just how much you really had indeed understood me and my need for direction and truly have allowed me the confidence and strength to know and believe I can achieve whatever I want in life"*

If you like natural products, hand-crafted gifts including Gemstone jewellery, objects of natural beauty – the finest examples from Mother Nature, tinged with an air of Mystery – then we will not disappoint you. For those who can enjoy that feeling of connection with the esoteric nature of Gemstones and Crystals, then our 'Power for Life – Power Bracelets could be ideal for you. Each bracelet comes with its own guide explaining a way of thinking that's so powerful it will change your life and the information comes straight from the Bible. e.g. read Mark 11: 22

We regularly give inspirational talks on Crystal Power – fact or fiction? A captivating story about the world's fascination with natural gemstones and crystals and how the Placebo effect explains the healing power of gemstones and crystals – it's intriguing. And it's available on a CD

To see our full range of books, jewellery and gifts including CD's and DVD'S

## Visit our web site - www.rosewood-gifts.co.uk

To see our latest videos go to 'You Tube' and type in Rosewood Gifts.